heart

heart

Barbara Chung

Canyon Wren Press
Santa Monica, California

Copyright © 2021 by Barbara Chung

All rights reserved. No part of this book may be used or performed without written consent from the author, if living, except for critical articles or reviews.

Canyon Wren Press
Santa Monica, California
www.canyonwrenpress.net

Cover design by Lluvia Arras

Heart / Barbara Chung – 1st edition
ISBN 978-1-7354489-3-0 (paperback)
ISBN 978-1-7354489-4-7 (eBook)

For inquiries, email hello@canyonwrenpress.net

Printed in the United States of America

For my friends, because you let me
chat with you in verse all the time

waterfall blossoms
will be a souvenir
for my drinking friends

—Matsuo Bashō
tr. Jane Reichhold

Contents

Preface ix

amazed 3
betrayed 4
blithe 5
charmed 6
comforted 7
contemptuous 8
creeped out 9
delighted 10
determined 11
disgusted 12
enchanted 13
furious 14

guarded   15
hopeful   16
indulgent   17
inspired   18
intrigued   19
lonely   20
pensive   21
restless   22
safe   23
thankful   24
wistful   25

Afterword   27
About the Author   29

Preface

This collection of verse began in conversations with friends.

I love the magical moments when unrelated elements form a relationship in my mind. This happens most often when talking with my friends, for they are vibrant, generous people who show me new perspectives. Gardens and boxing, jealousy and salsa, sailing and motherhood—imagine my surprise and delight when I realize odd pairings like these are not odd at all.

In such moments, I need to find words for these new associations. Short verse is often the fastest way to do so. Because my friends are also kind and patient, they've accepted my quirk of spouting verse spontaneously as we chat and my habit of creating poems from our conversations. This little book is for them.

The haikus enclosed here are about feelings, because we all have them, and because I trust my friends with mine. Haiku is a poetic form from Japanese tradition: three lines, with five, seven, and five syllables respectively. In 17 syllables, haiku often juxtaposes disparate images to evoke emotion and insight.

Look through these poems and see what my conversations with friends can become, for better or worse. Skip around as you wish; these haikus are not meant to be read in any particular order, not even the ones on the same page. I had so much fun writing these poems, and I hope you have fun reading them.

—B.C.

heart

amazed

have you heard the sound
of a butterfly's wings and
felt them brush your hand?

rose petals spill forth
their fragrance to soak the mist
woman in full bloom

ancient oak scorched black
green leaves offered through gnarled scars
man who starts anew

betrayed

you must be lying
I know, for I'm feline now
hair raised on arched back

∼

you love me best when
I break and clip me like a
bonsai when I grow

∼

soul of violet
did I make it up in my head
deaf to viper's tongue

blithe

lie under flowers
drink petal-tinted sunlight
see what the bugs see

crown of kingfishers
conspiracy of ravens
but swifts are just swifts

laughter seeking cause
to bubble up is better
than famous hot springs

charmed

so warm and so pouf
fat baby bear's pompadour
style icon so pure

∼

earnest sweet peas sprout
under wintertime grow lights
to dance in spring breeze

∼

golden retriever
offers fluffy paw to shake
pleasure to meet you

comforted

captain of her ship
she pilots her family
through cataclysm

on verge of tearfall
suddenly swaddled in warmth
soft dog with wet nose

unspeakable grief
acknowledged in spoken word
child receives a name

contemptuous

a selfish story
always the protagonist
never a hero

～

no thought in that mind
even a vacuum cleaner
holds what it picks up

～

girl you can keep him
no way am I putting my
chip in that salsa

creeped out

bat eyes blink from cave
he looks too closely and talks
too much and too near

cottontail rabbit
flees scene of its near capture
changing my mind now

her jealousy hides
but obsession oozes from
under closet door

delighted

the dark-eyed junco
peeks then hops through latticed fence
for lunch and chatter

∼

who is bouncier?
new tennis ball in play or
golden chasing it

∼

drink with true friends and
become bumblebees tumbling
into blossomed cups

determined

bobcat stalks her prey
walks slowly toward her pounce
I make my plans too

∼

hummingbird zooms to
storm-whipped blooms for it must eat
twice an hour or die

∼

young dudleya finds
sustenance in granite rocks
makes one leaf each month

disgusted

why did someone put
peas in the guacamole
must I be polite

~

I'm your favorite toy
to break, sad child, but I'm no
toy and you're a man

~

the world is burning
but you only allow small talk
petty arsonist

enchanted

barefoot in forest
new roots unfurl from my toes
wild roses from hair

gentle mallow births
coral flame and desert wind
in a city park

snowberries can grow
in shade because their own light
glows from deep within

furious

I flee the hills where
red-tailed hawks mesmerized me
only they may scream here

∼

O to hurl rocks like
the galaxy hurls them at earth
when shooting stars burn

∼

madwoman devours
what drove her mad and becomes
that which she consumes

guarded

trip wires, laser beams
timing devices, loaded springs
make for tiptoe talk

whack-a-mole isn't
any fun for the mole so
he forgoes fresh air

we take shallow breaths
as if to make asbestos
safer to inhale

hopeful

feisty flyweight plants
throw heavyweight punches with
flowers to save bees

∼

put fig tree sticks in
clean soil and await new roots
welcome immigrants

∼

moon hides sun from earth
sun inscribes shadows with moon
"see, earth? I'm still here"

indulgent

for sunset dinner
a cinnamon roll center
like the golden sun

∼

the fattest bear sits
in stream so salmon will swim
straight into his maw

∼

a whole bottle of
good champagne with tater tots
happy tipsy queen

inspired

thoughts glide on zephyr
blowing soap bubbles through sky
clean air, cleaner words

∼

pomegranate spills
seeds upon seeds, some rubies
others bleeding hearts

∼

those who choose kindness
when difficult send laughter
dancing through the hills

intrigued

earth's crust is thinner
than apple's peel, based on scale
I will step lightly

spiny new pupa
larva consuming itself
where does it begin?

dots and dashes on
alder bark would tell a tale
if we knew the code

lonely

no speckled stoneware
or French porcelain plates and bowls
just one plain white dish

∽

I drown as I breathe
the air where birds pour jeweled songs
too heavy to lift

∽

a sour companion
shrivels a fruitful spirit
late spring frost on vine

pensive

watering young plants
watering silence within
what will grow from it?

catharsis can drift
on the breeze like sagebrush seeds
set life in dry soil

fog winding through hills
coyotes howling unseen
singing to someone

restless

hungry princess finds
peas under mattress, couch, chair
everywhere but plate

∼

a small earthquake where
everything moves a little
nothing moves a lot

∼

child fidgets in chair
woman fidgets with her hair
life feels a bit unfair

safe

the ones who love me
wrap ten layers of pillows
unseen around me

tossed by my own waves
till a friend speaks truth that fits
like a life jacket

every journey ends
at home whether we return
or build one anew

thankful

home of books and plants
birthplace of happy memories
and happier dreams

～

the young valley oak
who knows only fire and drought
weaves a soft-leaved crown

～

gratitude becomes
water for the garden to
grow beyond its walls

wistful

under the old oak
our shared shadow veiling the
living and the dead

spent rose was once in
full bloom—that is still true though
seeds are hollow now

there isn't much time
so I watch for hours to not
miss what I will miss

Afterword

I wrote this poem inspired by a happy afternoon with cheddar & sour cream potato chips. While it is not a haiku, I still want to share it with you. Confession is part of friendship, after all.

This Is Just To Say
After William Carlos Williams

I have eaten
the big potato chip bag
I bought instead of
little bitty bags

because I care
for the earth our home
because I believe
I can eat just some

Forgive me
the bag was half empty
when I opened it
and the chips so crispy

About the Author

Barbara Chung is the author of the poetry collection *Sunlight*. Along with writing, she serves as a business strategy advisor and tends her garden, a certified wildlife habitat. She studied at Harvard University and University of California, Los Angeles. Barbara lives in Santa Monica, California.

www.ingramcontent.com/pod-product-compliance
Lightning Source LLC
Chambersburg PA
CBHW060346080526
44583CB00014B/1073